# When
## you
## consider
## the
## alternative

Chiefie!
This looks like
it should be the
Hallmark of our 70's.
Congratulations on getting
there first
before me

I 10'
Happy ol Big 10
Jeannie
10/27/96

by

Everybody

•••

collected by

William Cole

# WHEN YOU CONSIDER THE ALTERNATIVE

Enlightening

and Amusing

Words on Age

and Aging

St. Martin's Griffin
New York

A THOMAS DUNNE BOOK.
An imprint of St. Martin's Press.

Production Editor: David Stanford Burr

Design: Songhee Kim

Library of Congress Cataloging-in-Publication Data

When you consider the alternative : enlightening and amusing words
    on age and aging / edited by William Cole.—1st ed.
            p.    cm.
    ISBN 0-312-14445-8
    1. Aging—Humor.   2. Old age—Humor.   3. Aged—
Humor.   I. Cole, William.
PN6231.A43W44      1996
305.26—dc20                                            96-5996
                                                        CIP

First St. Martin's Griffin Edition: July 1996

10  9  8  7  6  5  4  3  2  1

..........................................

Old age isn't so bad

when you consider the

alternative

—**MAURICE CHEVALIER**, at 72

..........................

# CONTENTS •••••

T he English writer Nigel Nicolson wrote in his column in *The Spectator,* "There are five essentials for a happy old age, and I enjoy them all: good health, sufficient money, friendship (including family), congenial surroundings, and continued activity. I put the last first." Well now, I can see what he means, what with his living in Sissinghurst Castle, which comes with one of the great English gardens, and being a son of Sir Harold Nicolson, the aristocratic diplomat and diarist.

In a subsequent column he reports getting a letter from an eighty year old lady in Seattle, who comments that his list lacked a sixth benefit, at least for a woman, ". . . that one is no longer an object of sexual desire and jealousy." Humph! I agree with Mr. Nicolson but not with the old woman; sexual desire never goes, as many say in these pages. The performance may go, but not the desire.

Mr. Nicolson and I seem to share the approximate age—three score year and fifteen. Time enough to have found out the indignities the human body can go through; in my case the usual cataract operation, a couple of heart repairs, that fretsome and peculiar male inner part, the prostate. When faced with one of these procedures I said to the surgeon, "Y'know, I'm getting too old for this kind of caper." He answered, "In your seventies? That isn't old *these* days!"

No need for me to go on; I'll leave that to the following five hundred or so commentators. You've all read the poem "The Fairies" by William Allingham—the one that begins "Up the airy mountain, / Down the rushy glen." He wasn't always so fey, and had a quite cynical couplet that I've always admired:

> *Where do all the lovely children go to?*
> *Are these the stupid people that they grow to?*

············································

# When you consider the alternative

············································

# ALONG THE ROAD

● ● ● ● ● ● ● ● ● ● ● ● ● ● ● ● ● ●

"... too young to take

up golf and too old

to rush up to the net."

Years ago we discovered the exact point, the dead center of middle age. It occurs when you are too young to take up golf and too old to rush up to the net.

—FRANKLIN P. ADAMS

The young are slaves to dreams; the old, servants of regrets. Only the middle aged have all their five senses.

—HERVEY ALLEN

After age forty, it's patch, patch, patch all the way.

—anonymous

Middle age is a time of life that a man first notices in his wife.

—RICHARD ARMOUR

Nature gives you the face you have at twenty; it is up to you to merit the face you have at fifty.

—GABRIELLE "COCO" CHANEL

Pushing forty? She's clinging to it for dear life.

—IVY COMPTON-BURNETT

The children despise their parents until the age of forty, when they suddenly become just like them—thus preserving the system.

—**QUENTIN CREWE**

When a middle-aged man says in a moment of weariness that he is half dead, he is telling the literal truth.

—**ELMER DAVIS**

Middle-aged people may be divided into three classes: those who are still young, those who have forgotten they were young, and those who were never young.

—**VISCOUNT BERTRAND DAWSON,** Dawson of Penn

The great comfort of turning forty-nine is the realization that you are now too old to die young.

—**PAUL DICKSON**

By the time we hit fifty, we have learned our hardest lessons. We have found out that only a few things are really important. We have learned to take life seriously, but never ourselves.

—**MARIE DRESSLER**

After thirty, a man wakes up sad every morning, excepting perhaps five or six, until the day of his death.

—RALPH WALDO EMERSON

Setting a good example for your children takes all the fun out of middle age.

—WILLIAM FEATHER

At sixteen I was stupid, confused, insecure, and indecisive. At twenty-five I was wise, self-confident, prepossessing, and assertive. At forty-five I am stupid, confused, insecure, and indecisive. Who would have supposed that maturity is only a short break in adolescence?

—JULES FEIFFER

It is unthinkable for a Frenchman to arrive at middle age without having syphilis and the Cross of the Legion of Honor.

—ANDRÉ GIDE, recalled on his death

*She may very well pass for forty-three*
*in the dusk with a light behind her.*

—W. S. GILBERT

Whoever, in middle age, attempts to realize the wishes and hopes of his early youth, invariably deceives himself. Each ten years of a man's life has its own fortunes, its own hopes, its own desires.

—GOETHE

One's fifties can be giddy years, as anybody fifty knows. Chest pains, back pains, cancer scares, menopausal or prostate complications are not the least of it, and the fidelities of a lifetime, both personal and professional, may be called into question.

—EDWARD HOAGLAND

I was thinking, forty-five—that's middle age. Well, I'm going to have the best damn middle age anybody ever had.

—LAURA Z. HOBSON

[in middle age] Work is hard. Distractions are plentiful. And time is short.

—ADAM HOCHSCHILD

At middle age the soul should be opening up like a rose, not closing up like a cabbage.

—JOHN ANDREW HOLMES

The fifties is a kind of fulcrum decade, a turning point in the aging process during which people, more sharply than before, are made to feel their age.

—DR. DAVID KARP

Middle age is when you are sitting home on a Saturday night and the telephone rings and you hope it isn't for you.

—RING LARDNER

The real sadness of fifty is not that you change so much but that you change so little. . . . My only birthday resolution is to change some of my habits every year, even if for the worse.

—MAX LERNER

The long dull monotonous years of middle-aged prosperity or middle-aged adversity are excellent campaigning weather for the Devil.

—C. S. LEWIS

My age is thirty-nine plus tax.

—LIBERACE

Men who are orthodox when they are young are in danger of being middle-aged all their lives.

—**WALTER LIPPMANN**

Of middle age the best that can be said is that a middle-aged person has likely learned how to have a little fun in spite of his troubles.

—**DON MARQUIS**

The lovely thing about being forty is that you can appreciate twenty-five-year-old men more.

—**COLLEEN MCCULLOUGH**

How it rejoices a middle-aged woman when her husband criticizes a pretty girl!

—**MIGNON MCLAUGHLIN,** American aphorist

Middle age—by which I mean anything over twenty and under ninety.

—**A. A. MILNE**

I am in my fifties, and looking forward to the first glimmerings of my approach to the beginnings of the first foothills of early middle age.

—**FRANK MUIR**

*Forty-five isn't really old, it's right on the border,*
*At least, unless the elevator's out of order*

Middle age is when you have met so many people that every new person you meet reminds you of someone else and usually is.

—**OGDEN NASH**

Even though people in their fifties don't see themselves as old, there's a reversal of the direction of time. You count the number of birthdays left instead of how many you've reached.

—**DR. BERNICE NEUGARTEN,** psychologist

Middle age is when, whenever you go on holiday, you pack a sweater.

—**DENIS NORDEN**

At fifty everyone has the face he deserves.

—GEORGE ORWELL

Middle age is when anything new in the way you feel is most likely a symptom.

—LAURENCE J. PETER

Middle age is when you're faced with two temptations and you choose the one that will get you home by nine o'clock.

—RONALD REAGAN, on his 66th birthday

When I was young, I was told : "You'll see, when you're fifty." I am fifty and I haven't seen a thing.

—ERIK SATIE

An energetic middle life is, I think, the only safe precursor of a vitally happy old age.

—VIDA D. SCHUDDER

Forty was tough. Fifty you're already cruisin'. You better be. There ain't no way to stop it.

—SAM SHEPARD

# 2

# LOOKING OUT

• • • • • • • • • • • • • • • • • •

"...the most

unexpected of all

things to happen to a

man."

I think of myself as I was twenty-five years ago. Then I look in a mirror and see an old bastard and I realise it's me.

—**DAVE ALLEN,** Irish comedian

You don't grow old gradually, or on purpose, the way you go downtown on a subway. It's more like finding yourself standing in the last station wondering how you got there.

—**ROBERT THOMAS ALLEN**

Maturity is the day you have your first real laugh at yourself.

—**ETHEL BARRYMORE**

To me, old age is always fifteen years older than I am.

—**BERNARD BARUCH** on his 85th birthday

If I'd known I was gonna live this long, I'd have taken better care of myself.

—**EUBIE BLAKE,** age 100

The remembrance of their youth remains green in the heart of old men; they love the places where they lived; and the persons with whom they then began an acquaintance are dear to them; they still affect certain words in use when they first began to speak; they prefer the ancient style of singing and dancing; and boast of old fashions in dress, furnishing and carriages; they cannot bring themselves to disapprove of those things which served their passions, and are always recalling them. Can any one imagine these old men would prefer new customs and the latest fashions, which they do not adopt, and from which they have nothing to expect, which young men have invented, and which give them, in their turn, such a great advantage over their elders?

—JEAN DE LA BRUYÈRE,

Retirement at sixty-five is ridiculous. When I was sixty-five, I still had pimples.

—GEORGE BURNS

I feel age like an icicle down my back.

—DYSON CARTER

It is the misfortune of an old man that though he can put things out of his head he can't put them out of his feelings.

—JOYCE CARY

I am perhaps the oldest musician in the world, I am an old man but in many senses a very young man. And this is what I want you to be, young, young all your life, and to say things to the world that are true.

—**PABLO CASALS**, at 96

Statesmen and beauties are very rarely sensible of the gradations of their decay.

—**PHILIP STANHOPE**, Lord Chesterfield

The heart never grows better by age; I fear rather worse, always harder.

—**LORD CHESTERFIELD**

No one is so old that he does not think he could live another year.

—**CICERO**

In mirrors and especially in photographs, I notice that I have grown old. But it is what is young in me that notices it. It is a young man who sees an old one. He is amazed—without bitterness and with respect, the way youth regards old age among noble peoples. (In China, for instance.) My youth respects my old age. My old age protects my youth. That is why I am at peace.

—**JEAN COCTEAU**, at 62

I never feel old. I think every day that perhaps tomorrow I will stop being young and get down to work that is serious.

—SIR WILLIAM COLDSTREAM

The fear of aging, a commonplace neurosis, does not usually wait for age and spares neither sex.

—COLETTE

Oh Lord how old *old age* is. One doesn't (one *cannot*) conceive *how* old and awful old age is, till one is up to the eyes. *Then* . . . one says puff and blows it all out of the often empty windows.

—GORDON CRAIG

I don't believe one grows older. I think that what happens early on in life is that at a certain age one stands still and stagnates.

—T. S. ELIOT

Within I do not find wrinkles and used heart, but unspent youth.

—RALPH WALDO EMERSON, at 61

I'm not really a young man but I'm a man who's still young. Youth doesn't mean much. I'm very young, whereas all my contemporaries in Stampa are old men, because they've accepted old age. Their lives are already in the past. But mine is in the future. It's only now that I can envisage the possibility of trying to start on my life's work.

—ALBERTO GIACOMETTI

At times it seems that I am living my life backward, and that at the approach of old age my real youth will begin. My soul was born covered with wrinkles—wrinkles that my ancestors and parents most assiduously put there and that I had the greatest trouble removing, in some cases.

—ANDRÉ GIDE

I love everything that's old: old friends, old times, old manners, old books, old wines.

—OLIVER GOLDSMITH

To an old man any place that's warm is homeland.

—MAXIM GORKY

A person is always startled when he hears himself seriously called an old man for the first time.

—OLIVER WENDELL HOLMES JR.

An old codger, rampant, and still learning.

—ALDOUS HUXLEY

It is so comic to hear oneself called old, even at ninety, I suppose!

—ALICE JAMES

Growing old is a slow march into enemy territory.

—HENRY JAMES

Did you ever hear the story of a man who asked his physician whether he was not dangerously ill? "No sir, but you are dangerously old." So I too have come to the creaky places of life.

—BENJAMIN JOWETT

Once I was looking through the kitchen window at dusk and I saw an old woman looking in. Suddenly the light changed and I realized that the old woman was myself. You see, it all happens on the outside, inside one doesn't change.

—MOLLY KEANE, Irish Writer

The great secret that all old people share is that you really haven't changed in seventy or eighty years. Your body changes, but you don't change at all. And that, of course, causes great confusion.

—DORIS LESSING

I am luminous with age.

—MERIDAL LE SUER

Old Mr. Neave felt that he was too old for spring.

—KATHERINE MANSFIELD

The older I grow, the more I distrust the familiar doctrine that age brings wisdom.

—H. L. MENCKEN

*For ah, my heart! how very soon*
*The glittering dreams of youth are past!*
*And long before it reach its noon,*
*the sun of life is overcast.*

—GEORGE MOORE, "Elegiac Stanzas"

When you reach your sixties, you have decided whether you're going to be a sot or an ascetic. In other words if you want to go on working after you're sixty, some degree of asceticism is inevitable.

—MALCOLM MUGGERIDGE

Young people can seldom understand that at seventy-six one is very much the same person one was at twenty-five, just as the chairman finds no difficulty at all in identifying with the junior clerk he once was, while his colleagues cannot imagine him anything but chairman.

—NIGEL NICOLSON

After passing the half-century, one unavoidable conclusion is that many things seeming incredible starting out, are, in fact, by no means to be located in an area beyond belief.

—ANTHONY POWELL

There is more felicity on the far side of baldness than young men can possibly imagine.

—LOGAN PEARSALL SMITH

Being over seventy is like being engaged in a war. All our friends are going or gone and we survive amongst the dead and dying as on a battlefield.

—MURIEL SPARK

After the age of eighty, everything reminds you of something else.

—LOWELL THOMAS

The awareness of the ambiguity of one's highest achievements, as well as one's deepest failures, is a definite symptom of maturity.

—PAUL TILLICH

Old age is the most unexpected of all things to happen to a man.

—LEON TROTSKY

I am admonished in many ways that time is pushing me inexorably along. I am approaching the threshold of age; in 1977 I shall be 142. This is no time to be flitting about on earth. I must cease from the activities proper to youth and begin to take on the dignities and gravities and inertia proper to the season of honorable senility which is on its way.

—MARK TWAIN

Now that I am sixty, I see why the idea of elder wisdom has passed from currency.

—JOHN UPDIKE

One trouble with growing older is that it gets progressively tougher to find a famous historical figure who didn't amount to much when he was your age.

—**BILL VAUGHAN**

You all of a sudden realize that you are being ruled by people you went to high school with. You all of a sudden catch on that life is nothing but high school . . . class officers, cheerleaders, and all.

—**KURT VONNEGUT**

Old age is a special problem for me because I've never been able to shed the mental image I have of myself—a lad of about nineteen.

—**E. B. WHITE**

At my age, I take a certain comfortable satisfaction in easygoing negative decisions: *not* to raise certain questions in conversation, *not* to explain certain things. I am closer to the attitude recommended by [Benjamin] Jowett: never apologize, never explain. Why bother? I used to feel an obligation to correct people, to hold up my side. Now I don't feel that it matters. . . .

(at 73)

As a character in one of Chekov's plays says "He's a man of the eighties," so I find that I'm a man of the twenties. I still expect something exciting: drinks, animated conversation, gaiety: an uninhibited exchange of ideas. Scott Fitzgerald's idea that somewhere things were "glimmering."

—EDMUND WILSON

*I pray—for fashion's word is out*
*And prayer comes round again—*
*That I may seem, though I die old,*
*A foolish, passionate man.*

("A Prayer for Old Age")

*What shall I do with this absurdity*
*O heart, O troubled heart—this caricature*
*Decrepit old age that has been tied to me*
*As to a dog's tail.*

—WILLIAM BUTLER YEATS, "The Tower"

# 3

# LOOKED AT

●●●●●●●●●●●●●●●●

"...when a bastard

grows old, he simply

becomes an old

bastard."

All evil comes from the old. They grow fat on ideas and young men die of them.

—JEAN ANOUILH

There's only one thing worse than an old fogy, and that's a young fogy.

—TERREL BELL

You only have to survive in England and all is forgiven you . . . if you can eat a boiled egg at ninety in England they think you deserve a Nobel prize.

—ALAN BENNETT

I have never known a person to live to be one hundred and be remarkable for anything else.

—JOSH BILLINGS

The older you get in China, the more you're revered and respected and made a fuss of . . . whereas in the West we're more inclined to concentrate on getting the old folks out of our hair and into a nice little Eventide Home.

—BASIL BOOTHROYD

As favor and riches forsake a man, we discover in him the foolishness they concealed, and which no one perceived before.

—JEAN DE LA BRUYÈRE

To forge a fixed and arbitrary rule in terms of years as the limit of a man's usefulness or human service would only be to behead a large portion of the world's intellectual and moral leadership and thereby to impoverish mankind.

—NICHOLAS MURRAY BUTLER

There are three classes of elderly women; first, that dear old soul; second, that old woman; third, that old witch.

—SAMUEL TAYLOR COLERIDGE

When you win, you're an old pro. When you lose you're an old man.

—CHARLIE CONERLY, Quarterback, Giants Football Team

About sixty years ago, I said to my father, "Old Mr. Senex is showing his age; he sometimes talks quite stupidly." My father replied, "That isn't age. He's always been stupid. He is just losing his ability to conceal it."

—ROBERTSON DAVIES

Many a man that could't direct ye to th' drug store on th' corner when he was thirty will get a respectful hearin' when age has further impaired his mind.

—**Finley Peter Dunne**

To have lived long does not necessarily imply the gathering of much wisdom and experience. A man who has pedaled twenty-five thousand miles on a stationary bicycle has not circled the globe. He has only garnered weariness.

—**Paul Eldridge**

What a wretched lot of old shrivelled creatures we shall be by-and by. Never mind—the uglier we get in the eyes of others, the lovelier we shall be to each other; that has always been my firm faith about friendship.

—**George Eliot**

It does not become an old man to run after the fashion of the moment, either in thought or in dress. But he should know where he is, and what the others are aiming at.

—**Goethe**

When people tell you how young you look, they are also telling you how old you are.

—**Cary Grant**

In our memories people we no longer see age gracefully.

—GRAHAM GREENE

If you survive long enough, you're revered—rather like an old building.

—KATHARINE HEPBURN

You make me chuckle when you say that you are no longer young, that you have turned twenty-four. A man is or may be young to after sixty, and not old before eighty.

—OLIVER WENDELL HOLMES JR.

• • • • • • • • • • • •

No man is ever old enough to know better.

Don't try to convert the elderly person: circumvent him.

—HOLBROOK JACKSON

• • • • • • • • • • • •

There is a wicked inclination in most people to suppose an old man decayed in his intellects. If a young or middle-aged man, when leaving a company, does not recollect where he laid his hat, it is nothing; but if the same inattention is discovered in an old man, people will shrug their shoulders, and say, "His memory is going."

—**Samuel Johnson**

[W]e are as old or as young as other people make us feel.

—**Dr. David Karp**

Presently, I shall be introduced as "this venerable old gentleman" and the axe will fall when they raise me to the degree of "grand old man." This means on our continent anyone with snow-white hair who has kept out of jail till eighty.

—**Stephen Leacock**

They don't let me attend the board, but they allow me to come to lunch afterwards.

—**Harold Macmillian** at age 85, referring to his position as president of the firm

Few men of action have been able to make a graceful exit at the appropriate time.

—**Malcolm Muggeridge**

The quinquagenarian may not be master of himself, he is, notwithstanding, master of a passable miscellany of experience on which to draw when forming opinions, distorted or the reverse, at least up to a point of his own.

—ANTHONY POWELL

There are three periods in life: youth, middle age, and "how well you look."

—NELSON A. ROCKEFELLER

People seldom change as they age, they just get more as they always were.

—NED ROREM

Old men are dangerous; it doesn't matter to them what is going to happen to the world.

—GEORGE BERNARD SHAW

Men come of age at sixty, women at fifteen.

—JAMES STEPHENS

So much has been said and sung of beautiful young girls, why doesn't somebody wake up to the beauty of old women?

—HARRIET BEECHER STOWE

*Will you love me in December as you do in May,*
*Will you love me in the good old fashioned way?*
*When my hair has all turned gray,*
*Will you kiss me then and say,*
*That you love me in December as you do in May?*

—JAMES J. WALKER "Will You Love me in December as You do in May"

I delight in men over seventy, they always offer one the devotion of a lifetime.

—OSCAR WILDE Mrs. Allonby in *A Woman of No Importance*

There is an engaging legend abroad in the land that advancing years mellow one and somehow bring out the kindliest impulses of one's nature; that the countryside swarms with repentent Scrooges. My own observation has been that when a bastard grows old, he simply becomes an old bastard.

—ISABEL M. WILLETTS

At sixty you might come back; at seventy they think you are gaga.

—SIR HAROLD WILSON

I really believe that more harm is done by old men who cling to their influence than by young men who anticipate it.

—OWEN D. YOUNG

# 4

# THE

# GENERATION

# WAR

●●●●●●●●●●●●●●●●●●●●

"... a very high price

to pay for

maturity."

The old repeat themselves and the young have nothing to say. The boredom is mutual.

—JACQUES BAINVILLE

Young men think old men are fools; but old men know young men are fools.

—GEORGE CHAPMAN

I've always thought that the stereotype of the dirty old man is really the creation of a dirty young man who wants the field to himself.

—HUGH DOWNS

In the last few years everything I'd done up to sixty or so has seemed very childish.

—T. S. ELIOT

*Si jeunesse savoit, si vieillesse pouvoit.*
If youth but knew; if age but could.

—HENRI ESTIENNE II, French printer

In youth experience is unnecessary: in age we count on it and, generally speaking, only act successfully when it is to hand.

—E. M. FORSTER

When a man is young he is so wild he is insufferable. When he is old he plays the saint and becomes insufferable again.

—NIKOLAI GOGOL

Age looks with anger at the temerity of youth, and youth with contempt on the scrupulosity of age.

—SAMUEL JOHNSON

From the earliest times the old have rubbed it into the young that they are wiser than they, and before the young had discovered what nonsense this was they were old too, and it profited them to carry on the imposture.

—W. SOMERSET MAUGHAM

Youth has to do with spirit, not age. Men of seventy or eighty are often more youthful than the young. Theirs is the real youth.

—HENRY MILLER

The young have aspirations that never come to pass, the old have reminiscences of what never happened.

—H. H. MUNRO (SAKI)

The aged love what is practical, while impetuous youth longs only for what is dazzling.

—PETRARCH

*We think our fathers fools, so wise we grow;*
*Our wiser sons, no doubt, will think us so.*

—ALEXANDER POPE

If, as someone said, youth is a sickness that one spends the rest of his life trying to recover from, then surely old age is a classic case of the cure being worse than the disease.

—ARTHUR ROTH

It's all that the young can do for the old, to shock them and keep them up to date.

—GEORGE BERNARD SHAW

• • • • • • • • • • • •

It seemed so simple when one was young and new ideas were mentioned not to grow red in the face and gobble.

The denunciation of the young is a necessary part of the mental hygiene of elderly people, and greatly assists the circulation of their blood.

—LOGAN PEARSALL SMITH

• • • • • • • • • • • •

Nothing so dates a man as to decry the younger generation.

—ADLAI STEVENSON

All sorts of allowances are made for the illusions of youth; and none, or almost none, for the disenchantment of age.

—ROBERT LOUIS STEVENSON

I think age is a very high price to pay for maturity.

—TOM STOPPARD

A young man's ambition [is] to get along in the world and make a place for himself—half your life goes that way, till you're twenty-five or fifty. Then, if you're lucky, you make terms with life, you get released.

—ROBERT PENN WARREN

*Youth, large, lusty, loving—youth, full of grace, force, fascination.*
*Do you know that Old Age may come after you with equal grace, force, fascination?*

—WALT WHITMAN

# 5

# NEVER TOO OLD?

"...a disability to be

unchaste."

It is this very awareness that one is no longer an attractive object that makes life so unbearable for so many elderly people.

—SIMONE DE BEAUVOIR

Tranquillity comes with years, and that horrid thing which Freud calls sex is expunged.

—E. F. BENSON, author of the *Lucia* novels

If the devil were to offer me a resurgence of what is commonly called virility, I'd decline. "Just keep my liver and lungs in good working order," I'd reply, "so I can go on drinking and smoking."

—LUIS BUÑUEL

I'm at the age now where just putting my cigar in its holder is a thrill.

—GEORGE BURNS

To grow old is to pass from passion to compassion.

—ALBERT CAMUS

Old men are like that, you know. It makes them feel important to think they are in love with somebody.

*Filth and old age, I'm sure you will agree,*
*Are powerful wardens upon chastity.*

—CHAUCER, "Wife of Bath's Tale"

Oh, to be seventy again!

—GEORGES CLEMENCEAU, on seeing a pretty girl on his 80th birthday.

Chastity is not chastity in an old man, but a disability to be unchaste.

—JOHN DONNE

Older women are best because they always think they may be doing it for the last time.

—IAN FLEMING

When you cease to be delicious you get dumped.

—KATHERINE HEPBURN

The older you get, the easier it is to resist temptation, but the harder it is to find.

—**Dr. Joseph H. Humpert**

[T]here are few things that we so unwillingly give up, even in advanced age, as the supposition that we still have the power of ingratiating ourselves with the fair sex.

—**Samuel Johnson**

A man's only as old as the woman he feels.

—**Groucho Marx**

*The girl who felt my stare and raised her eyes*
*Saw I was only an old man, and looked away*
*As people do when they see something not quite nice.*

—**T. S. Matthews**, "Name and Address"

She was twenty years younger than I was, and at forty-six or thereabouts one begins to feel that one's time for love is over; one is consultant rather than practitioner.

—**George Moore**

I used to have four supple members and one stiff one. Now I have four stiff ones and one supple one.

—Duc Charles Auguste Louis Joseph de Morny

In mid-life the man wants to see how irresistible he still is to younger women. How they turn their hearts to stone and more or less commit a murder of their marriage I just don't know, but they do.

—Patricia Neal, American actress

The assumption of the young that they are no longer objects of desire to the old is not true, but it is a convenient myth.

—Nigel Nicolson

Someone asked Sophocles, "How do you feel about sex? Are you still able to have a woman?" He replied, "Hush, man; most glad indeed I am to be rid of it all, as though I had escaped from a mad and savage master."

—Plato

• • • • • • • • • • • •

It is said of me that when I was young I divided my time impartially among wine, women, and song. I deny this categorically. Ninety percent of my interests were women.

When I was young, I used to have successes with women because I was young. Now I have successes with women because I am old. Middle age was the hardest part.

—**ARTHUR RUBINSTEIN**

How unnatural the imposed view, imposed by a puritanical ethos, that passionate love belongs only to the young, that people are dead from the neck down by the time they are forty, and that any deep feeling, any passion after that age, is either ludicrous or revolting!

—**MAY SARTON**

*As I grow older and older*
*And totter towards the tomb*
*I find that I care less and less*
*Who goes to bed with whom.*

—**DOROTHY L. SAYERS**

When men grow virtuous in their old age, they only make a sacrifice to God of the devil's leavings.

—**JONATHAN SWIFT**

To see a young couple loving each other is no wonder; but to see an old couple loving each other is the best sight of all.

—**WILLIAM MAKEPEACE THACKERAY**

An old man marrying a young girl is like buying a book for some one else to read.

—**H. W. THOMPSON**

From thirty-five to forty-five women are old, and at forty-five the devil takes over, and they're beautiful, splendid, maternal, proud. The acidities are gone, and in their place reigns calm. They are worth going out to find, and because of them some men never grow old. When I see them my mouth waters.

—**JEAN-BAPTISTE TROIGROS**, restaurateur

For certain people, after fifty, litigation takes the place of sex.

—**GORE VIDAL**

When you are as old as I, young man, you will know that there is only one thing in the world worth living for, and that is sin.

—**JANE WILDE**, Oscar's mother, in her 60s

At sixty . . . the sexual preoccupation, when it hits you, seems somewhat sharper, as if it were an elderly malady, like gout.

—**EDMUND WILSON**

*It's never too late to have a fling*
*For autumn is just as nice as spring*
*And it's never too late to fall in love.*

—**SANDY WILSON,** *The Boy Friend*

The older one grows the more one likes indecency.

—**VIRGINIA WOOLF**

# 6

# Signs and Portents

● ● ● ● ● ● ● ● ● ● ● ● ● ● ● ● ● ●

"... how young the

policemen look."

All the best sands of my life are somehow getting into the wrong end of the hourglass. If I could only reverse it! Were it in my power to do so, would I?

—THOMAS BAILEY ALDRICH

I don't want to be the oldest performer in captivity. . . . I don't want to look like a little old man dancing out there.

—FRED ASTAIRE

Take a close-up of a woman past sixty! You might as well use a picture of a relief map of Ireland!

—VISCOUNTESS NANCY ASTOR

A man is not old until regrets take the place of dreams.

—JOHN BARRYMORE

The worst thing about old age is having to get dressed and undressed every day.

—HILAIRE BELLOC

I hope I never get so old I get religious.

—INGMAR BERGMAN

• • • • • • • • • • • •

I smoke ten to fifteen cigars a day. At my age I have to hold on to something.

You know you're old when you bend down to tie your shoe and you wonder what else you can do while you're down there.

—GEORGE BURNS

• • • • • • • • • • • • •

It is the ugliness of old age that I hate. Being old is not bad if you keep away from mirrors; but broken-down feet, bent knees, peering eyes, rheumatic knuckles, withered skin, these are *ugly*, hard to tolerate with patience.

—EMILY CARR

A day's endless when you're young, whereas when you grow old it's very soon over. When you're retired, a day's a flash, when you're a kid it's very slow.

—LOUIS-FERDINAND CÉLINE

Let's go out and buy playing cards, good wine, bridge-scorers, knitting needles—all the paraphernalia to fill a gaping void, all that's required to disguise that monster, an old woman.

—COLETTE

The real curse of being old is the ejection from a citizen-ship traditionally based on work.

—DR. ALEX COMFORT

I have a horrible dislike of old age. Everybody's dead—half, no nearly all of one's contemporaries—and those that aren't are gaga. Someone rang the other day and said, "I want to invite you and Duff over for dinner." I said, "But Duff's been dead for over twenty-eight years."

—LADY DIANA COOPER

After the age of fifty we begin to die little by little in the death of others.

—JULIO CORTÁZAR

Put cotton in your ears and pebbles in your shoes. Pull on rubber gloves. Smear Vaseline over your glasses, and there you have it: instant old age.

—MALCOLM COWLEY

Nothing ages a man like living always with the same woman.

—NORMAN DOUGLAS

I never dared be radical when young for fear it would make me conservative when old.

—ROBERT FROST

Old age is when you look the food over, instead of the waitress.

—HY GARDNER

You know, when I first went into the movies Lionel Barrymore played my grandfather. Later he played my father and finally he played my husband. If he had lived, I'm sure I would have played his mother. That's the way it is in Hollywood. The men get younger and the women get older.

—LILLIAN GISH

The first sign of his approaching end was when my old aunts, while undressing him, removed a toe with one of his socks.

—GRAHAM GREENE

We have not passed that subtle line between childhood and adulthood until we move from the passive voice to the active voice—that is, until we have stopped saying "It got lost," and say "I lost it."

—SYDNEY J. HARRIS

You will recognize, my boy, the first sign of old age: it is when you go out into the streets of London and realize for the first time how young the policemen look.

—SIR SEYMOUR HICKS

I seem to be all right now. I stoop but I haven't lumbago. The doctor said little processes like icicles had grown from my spine and there was nothing to do but grin and bear it. Don't you wish you had icicles growing from your vertebrae?

—OLIVER WENDELL HOLMES JR.

I don't feel eighty. In fact I don't feel anything till noon. Then it's time for my nap.

—BOB HOPE

Physically, I face the normal problems of my age. Familiar obstacles such as stairs, whose ubiquitous presence I once took for granted, have become my enemies; they have forced me into a new reliance upon railings and banisters, for which I feel the same resentment as I have long felt toward the eyeglasses, hearing aids, and other mechanical devices upon which I am increasingly dependent.

—JOHN HOUSEMAN

Age makes eagles lose their feathers, makes old fogeys' footsteps fail, sets an old crone's teeth decaying, gives an old man withered hands—and they all get withered souls.

—**HENRIK IBSEN**

But our Machines have now been running seventy or eighty years, and we must expect that, worn as they are, here a pivot, there a wheel, now a pinion, next a spring, will be giving way; and however we may tinker with them up for a while, all will at length surcease motion.

—**THOMAS JEFFERSON**, at 71, in a letter to John Adams, 78

My diseases are an asthma and a dropsy and, what is less curable, seventy-five.

—**SAMUEL JOHNSON**

I will never grow old. My hands will never be discolored with spots of age. I will never have varicose veins. My balls will never become pendulous, hanging down as old men's balls do. My penis will never be shriveled. My legs will never be spindly, My belly, never big and heavy. My shoulders never stooped, rounded. . . . My face will never wrinkle. . . . My teeth will never yellow. . . . Bill T. Jones will never grow old.

—**BILL T. JONES**, dancer and choreographer

I am Retired Leisure. I am to be met with in trim gardens. I am already come to be known by my vacant face and careless gesture, perambulating at no fixed pace nor with any settled purpose. I walk about; not to and from.

—CHARLES LAMB

How is it that our memory is good enough to retain the least triviality that happens to us, and yet not good enough to recollect how often we have told it to the same person?

—LA ROCHEFOUCAULD

I have everything now I had twenty years ago—except now it's all lower.

—GYPSY ROSE LEE

If God had to give a woman wrinkles, He might at least have put them on the soles of her feet.

—NINON DE LENCLOS

It has been said that there is no fool like an old fool, except a young fool. But the young fool has first to grow up to be an old fool to realize what a damn fool he was when he was a young fool.

—HAROLD MACMILLAN

The worst thing about old age is the rapidity with which your periphery sinks.

—**DOROTHY REED MENDENHALL**

Time has the same effect on the mind as on the face; the predominant passion and the strongest feature become more conspicuous from the others' retiring.

—**LADY MARY WORTLEY MONTAGU**

I am becoming fatter and developing a paunch. I notice that it affects the way I walk. I move more slowly, and with a swinging movement, like an elephant. It is dreadful when one notices in oneself the movements and gait of an old man.

—**HAROLD NICOLSON,** at 64

Legend would have it that we, the elderly, are deaf . . . but nothing could be further from the truth. What we do find is that few people speak up as they used to.

—**C. NORTHCOTE PARKINSON**

Good cheekbones are the brassiere of old age.

—**BARBARA DE PORTAGO**

As the eighth decade gradually consumes itself, shadows lengthen, a masked and muffled figure loiters persistently at the back of every room as if waiting for a word at the most tactful moment, a presence more easily discerning than heretofore that exhales undoubted menace yet also extends persuasive charm of an enigmatic kind.

—ANTHONY POWELL

A woman is as young as her knees.

—MARY QUANT

Old age is a bed full of bones.

—JOHN RAY

First you forget names, then you forget faces; then you forget to zip your fly, then you forget to unzip your fly.

—BRANCH RICKEY

There are people whose watch stops at a certain hour and who remain permanently at that age.

—CHARLES AUGUSTIN SAINTE-BEUVE

Have you not a moist eye? a dry hand? a yellow cheek? a white beard? a decreasing leg? an increasing belly? is not your voice broken? your wind short? your chin double? your wit single? and every part about you blasted with antiquity?

—**WILLIAM SHAKESPEARE** *2 Henry IV* I.ii

A man is as old as his arteries.

—**THOMAS SYDENHAM**

Sleeping as quiet as death, side by wrinkled side, toothless, salt brown, like two old kippers in a box.

—**DYLAN THOMAS**

With sixty staring me in the face, I have developed inflammation of the sentence structure and a definite hardening of the paragraphs.

—**JAMES THURBER**

My legs have become very ugly. But then, what use would beautiful legs be to a woman of eighty-five?

—**DAME REBECCA WEST**

*At my age [65],* I find that I alternate between spells of fatigue and indifference when I am almost ready to give up the struggle, and spells of expanding ambition, when I feel that I can do more than ever before.

—EDMUND WILSON

Now I'm over sixty I'm veering toward respectability.

—SHELLEY WINTERS

I began to realize that I am growing old: The taxi driver calls me "Pop" instead of "Buddy."

—ALEXANDER WOOLLCOTT

# 7

# THE GOOD . . .

• • • • • • • • • • • • • • • • • •

"... then you are

wonderful."

I used to dread getting older because I thought I would not be able to do all the things I wanted to do, but now that I am older I find that I don't want to do them.

—**VISCOUNTESS NANCY ASTOR**, on her 80th birthday

[A]s I must leave off being young, I find many Douceurs in being a sort of Chaperon, for I am put on the Sofa near the fire & can drink as much wine as I like.

—**JANE AUSTEN**

While everything else physical and mental seems to diminish, the appreciation of beauty is on the increase. Landscapes, animals, men, women and children, and all man-made things fascinate, delight, and evoke my critical sense more and more.

—**BERNARD BERENSON**, at 85

Old age is like climbing a mountain. You climb from ledge to ledge. The higher you get, the more tired and breathless you become, but your view becomes much more extensive.

—**INGMAR BERGMAN**

But people keep hopeful and warm and *loving* right to the end—with much more to endure than I endure.—I see the old constantly, on these uptown streets—and they are not "depressed." Their eyes are bright; they have bought themselves groceries; they gossip and laugh—with, often, crippling handicaps evident among them.

—LOUISE BOGAN

Old age takes away from us what we have inherited and gives us what we have earned.

—GERALD BRENAN

Perhaps one has to be very old before one learns to be amused rather than shocked.

—PEARL S. BUCK

It is not all bad, this getting old, ripening. After the fruit has got its growth it should juice up and mellow. God forbid I should live long enough to ferment and rot and fall to the ground in a squash.

—EMILY CARR

Age has its compensations. It is less apt to be browbeaten by discretion.

—CHARLIE CHAPLIN

When Winston Churchill became prime minister he was overy sixty-five years old, already qualified for an old-age pension.

—JOHN COLVILLE

Autumn has always been my favorite season, and evening has been for me the pleasantest time of day. I love the sunlight but I cannot fear the coming of the dark.

—ALFRED DUFF COOPER

First you are young; then you are middle-aged; then you are old; then you are wonderful.

—LADY DIANA COOPER

"Don't worry about senility," my grandfather used to say. "When it hits you, you won't know it."

—BILL COSBY

They tell you that you'll lose your mind when you grow older. What they don't tell is the you won't miss it very much.

—MALCOLM COWLEY

Just as a cowherd drives, with his staff, the cows into the pasture, so old age and death drive us into a new existence.

—The **DHAMMAPADA**, probably 3rd century B.C.

I really believe—and it isn't just the desire to think it— that getting old is an adventure. If you've managed to keep your marbles—and my wife and I are in very good health—that there are all sorts of things going for it. You're balancing your books, waiting to present your final accounts.

—**ROBERTSON DAVIES**, at 78

After the age of eighty, all contemporaries are friends.

—**MME. DE DINO**

I've always thought that very few people grow old as admirably as academics. At least books never let them down.

—**MARGARET DRABBLE**

The love we have in our youth is superficial compared to the love that an old man has for his old wife.

—**WILL DURANT**

My feelings are those of a schoolboy getting in sight of the holidays. Or more seriously, my feelings are perhaps those of a matador who has decided not to enter the bull ring.

—**GEOFFREY FISHER**, Archbishop of Canterbury, planning to retire

What a relief at this age, finally, that I don't have to compete to prove myself—that I can live with the fact that I'll never rappel and that failure doesn't really matter one way or another.

—**BETTY FRIEDAN**, refusing to descend a 300-foot cliff with Outward Bound

Old age is the happiest time in a man's life. The worst of it is, there's so little of it.

—**W. S. GILBERT**

To grow older is a new venture in itself.

—**GOETHE**

I am in the prime of senility.

—**JOEL CHANDLER HARRIS**

Old age, believe me, is a good and pleasant thing. It is true you are gently shouldered off the stage, but then you are given such a comfortable front stall as spectator.

—**Jane Harrison**

To be seventy years young is sometimes far more cheerful and hopeful than to be forty years old.

—**Oliver Wendell Holmes Jr.**

Every man's memory is his private literature.

—**Aldous Huxley**

As one grows older, one becomes wiser and more foolish.

—**La Rochefoucauld**

I believe that one has to be seventy before one is full of courage. The young are always half-hearted.

—**D. H. Lawrence**

All one's life as a young woman one is on show, a focus of attention, people notice you. You set yourself up to be noticed and admired. And then, not expecting it, you become middle-aged and anonymous. No one notices you. You achieve a wonderful freedom. It is a positive thing. You can move about, unnoticed and invisible.

—**DORIS LESSING**

It seems a token and habit of older age to feel very deeply the charm there is in every display of life: I love it yearly more and more—in the antics and questions of children, in the roaming of a baby's surprised eyes, in the sparrow (now as I write) cracking seeds on the balcony . . . in the white shimmer of apple-blossom I saw yesterday at Clamart, and in the garden there in the dusk, when we walked under the chestnuts.

—**STEPHEN MACKENNA**

I think I'm the Picasso of mime. At eighty, Picasso was young. If I keep my fitness, I have at least another ten years. It's an encouragement for all men in their fifties, sixties, and seventies. I don't think of age. I think of life force and creation.

—**MARCEL MARCEAU**, at 70

Between the years of ninety-two and a hundred and two, we shall be the ribald, useless drunken, outcast person we have always wished to be. We shall have a long white beard and long white hair; we shall not walk at all, but recline in a wheel chair and bellow for alcoholic beverages; in the winter we shall sit before the fire with our feet in a bucket of hot water. and a decanter of corn whisky near at hand, and write ribald songs against organized society.

—Don Marquis

Growing old is something you do if you're lucky.

—Groucho Marx

The complete life, the perfect pattern, includes old age as well as youth and maturity. The beauty of the morning and the radiance of noon are good, but it would be a very silly person who drew the curtains and turned on the light in order to shut out the tranquility of the evening. Old age has its pleasures, which, though different, are not less than the pleasures of youth.

—W. Somerset Maugham

I must confess, with sixty only around the corner, that I have found existence on this planet extremely amusing, and, taking one day with another, perfectly satisfactory. If I had my life to live over again I don't think I'd change it in any particular of the slightest consequence.

—H. L. MENCKEN

There is no such thing as an old woman. Any woman of any age, if she loves, if she is good, gives a man a sense of the infinite.

—JULES MICHELET

You have to have other interests in life besides your own face, your own past. I try to see aging as a privilege. Aging allows me to do anything I want. It gives me freedom to speak up and tell the truth.

—JEANNE MOREAU

One of the many pleasures of old age is giving things up.

—MALCOLM MUGGERIDGE

"Beautiful is youth, it never comes again," goes the German saying. I beg to amend it by by inserting "because" just after the comma. Youth is a nuisance. Only very old men become gaga lamenting that it is no longer theirs.

—GEORGE JEAN NATHAN

The advantage of a bad memory is that one can enjoy good things for the first time several times.

—FRIEDRICH W. NIETZSCHE

Here, with whitened hair, desires falling, strength ebbing out of him, with the sun gone down and with only the serenity and calm warming of the evening star left to him, he drank to Life, to what it was, to what it would be. Hurrah!

—SEAN O'CASEY

Religion often gets credit for curing rascals when old age is the real medicine.

—AUSTIN O'MALLEY

I am amazed that life seems to get more and more interesting as one gets older—and also perhaps saner, serener, more tough. It is no doubt the Indian Summer before the hand of decrepitude strikes and health crumbles.

—FRANCES PARTRIDGE

• • • • • • • • • • •

One of the delights known to age, and beyond the grasp of youth, is that of Not Going.

After seven we start disinheriting ourselves, and after seventy, with any luck, we begin to unload a lot of damned rubbish that has been weighing us down for fifty-odd years.

[F]or thousands of generations not only were the old able to cope with the world but it was agreed that it was they who were better able to cope than anybody else. They were in fact respectfully consulted as experienced copers. Grandfather was not a problem but a solver of problems. And clearly there is much to be said in favour of societies that honoured old age and did not put all the emphasis on youth.

—J. B. PRIESTLY

Retirement must be wonderful. I mean, you can suck in your stomach for only so long.

—BURT REYNOLDS

The thing is that when one's old, in the sunset of one's life—the best time for richness of color and light—one requires a new approach to everything, and especially to affection. . . . When you feel your own "self" getting less intense, you love people and things for what they are in themselves, and what they represent in the eyes of your soul, and not for what they will contribute to your own destiny.

—GEORGE SAND

*Old age is not an illness, it is a timeless ascent.*
*As power diminishes, we grow towards the light.*

—**MAY SARTON,** "The Family of Woman"

Time and trouble will tame an advanced young woman, but an advanced old woman is uncontrollable by any earthly force.

—**DOROTHY L. SAYERS**

Age puzzles me. I thought it was a quiet time. My seventies were interesting and fairly serene, but my eighties are passionate. I grow more intense as I age.

—**FLORIDA SCOTT-MAXWELL**

How are you? I have come through the shadows and am enjoying a hardy and unscrupulous old age in insufferable celebrity.

—**GEORGE BERNARD SHAW,** letter to Irish friend

• • • • • • • • • • •
Growing old is no gradual decline, but a series of tumbles, full of sorrow, from one ledge to another. Yet when we pick ourselves up we find no bones are broken; while not unpleasing is the new terrace which stretches out unexplored before us.

How can they say my life is not a success? Have I not for more than sixty years got enough to eat and escaped being eaten?

An evil name—a drawback at first—sheds luster on old age.

We grow with years more fragile in body, but morally stouter, and can throw off the chill of a bad conscience almost at once.

The mere process of growing old together will make the slightest acquaintance seem a bosom friend.

—LOGAN PEARSALL SMITH

From the ages of thirteen to fifty society places women in a defined role.—At fifty, we leave it, and at sixty, we've completed the transition.—Assuming that we have a little security, we are now totally free to be ourselves. We're back to that stage of being a little girl of nine or ten, who can climb trees and be autonomous. . . . But we have our own apartments.

—GLORIA STEINEM

By the time a man gets well into his seventies his continued existence is a mere miracle.

—ROBERT LOUIS STEVENSON

If you live long enough, the venerability factor creeps in: you get accused of things you never did and praised for virtues you never had.

—I. F. STONE

A cultivated woman—a woman of breeding and intelligence—can enrich a man's life immeasurably. I have those things to offer, and time doesn't take them away. Physical beauty is passing—a transitory possession—but beauty of the mind, richness of the spirit, tenderness of the heart—I have all those things—aren't taken away but grow! Increase with the years!

—TENNESSEE WILLIAMS Blanche Dubois in *Streetcar Named Desire*

• • • • • • • • • • • •

Reading that Goethe wrote almost all the Second Part of *Faust* between the ages of seventy-three and eighty-six has somewhat stimulated and cheered me up.

(at age 70)

Old fogyism is comfortably closing in.

—EDMUND WILSON

• • • • • • • • • • • •

**8**

# And the

# bad . . .

• • • • • • • • • • • • • • • •

"You can't even take

salt for granted."

When you're forty, half of you belongs to the past—and when you are seventy, nearly all of you.

—**JEAN ANOUILH**

"I am seventy-five. Nothing is as much fun as it used to be."

—**JOHN BARRYMORE,** when asked if acting was as much fun as it used to be

The utmost span of a man's life is a hundred years. Half of it is spent in night, and of the rest half is lost by childhood and old age. Work, grief, longing, and illness make up what remains.

—The **BHARTRIHARI**

Old age is . . . a lot of crossed off names in an address book.

To be old is to be part of a huge and ordinary multitude . . . the reason why old age was venerated in the past because it was extraordinary.

—**RONALD BLYTHE**

There is nothing sadder than an old hipster.

—**LENNY BRUCE**

*What is the worst of woes that wait on age?*
*What stamps the wrinkle deeper on the brow?*
*To view each loved one blotted from life's page,*
*And be alone on earth, as I am now.*

—**LORD BYRON**, *Childe Harold's Pilgrimmage*

*And we who once rang out like a bell*
*Have nothing now to show or to sell;*
*Old bones to carry, old stories to tell;*
*So it be to an Old Soldier.*

—**PADRAIC COLUM**, "Old Soldier"

Old age is life's parody.

Never, on any plane, does the aged person lapse into a "second childhood," since childhood is, by definition a forward, upward movement.

—**SIMONE DE BEAUVOIR**

Old age is a shipwreck.

—**CHARLES DE GAULLE**

Regrets are the natural property of grey hairs.

—CHARLES DICKENS

As we grow old we slowly come to believe that everything will turn out badly for us, and that failure is in the nature of things; but then we do not much mind what happens to us one way or the other.

—ISAK DINESEN

Youth is a blunder; manhood a struggle, old age a regret.

—BENJAMIN DISRAELI

When you've been used to doing things, and they've been taken away from you, it's as if your hands had been cut off.

—GEORGE ELIOT

The years between fifty and seventy are the hardest. You are always being asked to do things, and you are not yet decrepit enough to turn them down.

—T. S. ELIOT

Grow up, and that is a terribly hard thing to do. It is much easier to skip it and go from one childhood to another.

—F. SCOTT FITZGERALD

My vitality goes more and more in keeping myself young.
When I was young it went in creating.

—**E. M. FORSTER,** at 51

It cannot be called fun in anybody's vocabulary.

—**KATHERINE HEPBURN**

He that is not handsome at twenty, nor strong at thirty,
nor rich at forty, nor wise at fifty, will never be handsome,
strong, rich, or wise.

—**GEORGE HERBERT**

What a drag it is getting old.

—**MICK JAGGER** and **KEITH RICHARDS** from their song,
"Mother's Little Helper"

How can a moribund old man reason back to himself the
romance, the mystery, the imminence of great things with
which our old earth tingled for him in the days when he
was young and well?

—**WILLIAM JAMES**

The ultimate indignity is to be given a bedpan by a
stranger who calls you by your first name.

—**MAGGIE KUHN**

Old age, where desire remains intact but hope extinct, where the fountains of pleasure run dry, and pain grows always greater, and good is no longer granted.

—GIACOMO LEOPARDI

Often I have wished myself dead, but [I do so] well under my blanket, so that neither death nor man could hear me.

—GEORG CHRISTOPH LICHTENBERG

*Whatever poet, orator, or sage*
*May say of it, old age is still old age.*

—HENRY WADSWORTH LONGFELLOW

[O]ne of the chief dangers of senectitude is a contented nestling of tastes and opinions formed many years ago, and of necessity steadily narrowing . . .

—GEORGE LYTELLTON

*Gone to grass, gone to grass!*
*He roared like a bull, he brayed like an ass,*
*He fed on beans and garden sass,*
*And he's gone to grass, he's gone to grass!*

—DON MARQUIS

You can't even take salt for granted.

—GROUCHO MARX

It's a hell of an ambition, wanting to be mellow. It's like wanting to be senile.

—RANDY NEWMAN

Oh dear! How age creeps up on one, slouch, slough, slop. Not a winged chariot but like an old pedlar in snow-boots which are too big for him.

—HAROLD NICOLSON

One starts to get young at the age of sixty and then it is too late.

—PABLO PICASSO

Growing old is like being increasingly penalized for a crime you haven't committed.

—ANTHONY POWELL

It is better to die young than to outlive all whom one loved, and all that rendered one lovable.

—MARGUERITE POWER, Countess of Blessington

As you become older you become more boring and better behaved.

—SIMON RAVEN

My approach to growing older is one of hysterical denial. I don't go for that growing-old-gracefully-the-best-is-yet-to-be con game. I intend to grow old bitterly, meanly, viciously.

—**ARTHUR ROTH**

• • • • • • • • • • •

Nothing can be meaner than the anxiety to live on, to live on anyhow and in any shape.

I sometimes think we all die at twenty-five and after that are nothing but walking corpses, with gramophones inside.

—**GEORGE SANTAYANA**
• • • • • • • • • • •

Is there anything worse than beginning to live when you are old?

—**SENECA**

• • • • • • • • • • • •

*I am a very foolish, fond old man,*
*Fourscore and upward, not an hour more or less;*
*And, to deal plainly,*
*I fear I am not in my perfect mind.*

(*King Lear* IV.vii)

*For you and I are past our dancing days.*

*(Romeo and Juliet* I.v)


*Golden lads and girls all must,*
*As chimney-sweepers, come to dust.*

—**WILLIAM SHAKESPEARE,** *Cymbeline* IV.ii

One evil in old age is that, as your time is come, you think every little illness the beginning of the end. When a man expects to be arrested, every knock on the door is an alarm.

—**SYDNEY SMITH**

After a certain distance, every step we take in life we find the ice growing thinner below our feet, and all around us and behind us we see our contemporaries going through.

—**ROBERT LOUIS STEVENSON**

Old age is a time of humiliations, the most disagreeable of which, for me, is that I cannot work long at sustained high pressure with no leaks in concentration.

—**IGOR STRAVINSKY**

Anyway, I'd be too old for you. "Cold are the hands of time that creep along relentlessly, destroying slowly but without pity that which yesterday was young. Alone, our memories resist the disintegration and grow more lovely with the passing years." That's hard to say with false teeth.

—**ROBERT DUDLEY** to **CLAUDETTE COLBERT** in
Preston Sturges's *The Palm Beach Story*.

The greatest problem about old age is the fear that it may go on too long.

—**A. J. P. TAYLOR**

I hope I die before I get old.

—**PETE TOWNSHEND**

Old age is like a worn-out dressing gown; it shames us to wear it, yet we cannot bring ourselves to throw it away.

—**PËTR VYÁZEMSKY**

Old age is a curious thing. It leaves a man crawling like a beetle while his mind is as strong and young as ever.

—**EVELYN WAUGH**

It is a terrible thing for an old woman to outlive her dogs.

—**TENNESSEE WILLIAMS**

When you retire . . . you go from Who's Who to who's that? . . .

—Citibank CEO **WALTER B. WRISTON** on retiring

# 9

# OBSERVATIONS

"... the only disease

that you don't look

forward to being

cured of."

Do not resist growing old—many are denied the privilege.

> *As men draw near the common goal*
> *Can anything be sadder*
> *Than he who, master of his soul*
> *Is servant to his bladder?*

—anonymous

If I had my life to live over again, I would start barefoot earlier in the spring.

—anonymous 85-year-old woman

Age has a good mind and sorry shanks.

—PIETRO ARETINO

Men of age object too much, consult too long, adventure too little, repent too soon, and seldom drive business home to the full period, but content themselves with a mediocrity of success.

—FRANCIS BACON

An old man looks permanent, as if he had been born an old man.

—H. E. BATES

We grow neither better nor worse as we get old, but more like ourselves.

—MAY LAMBERTON BECKER

A man of eighty has outlived probably three new schools of painting, two of architecture and poetry, a hundred in dress.

—JOYCE CARY

An archaeologist is the best husband any woman can have; the older she gets, the more interested he is in her.

—AGATHA CHRISTIE

You could say people are living longer because of the decline in religion. Not many people believe in the hereafter, so they keep going.

—DR. CYRIL CLARKE

The aging male actor's chief worry is his hairline; the female, her broad bottom.

—WILLIAM ROSSA COLE

As we grow older . . . we discover that the lives of most human beings are worthless except in so far as they contribute to the enrichment and emancipation of the spirit. . . . No one over thirty-five is worth meeting who has not something to teach us—something more than we could learn by ourselves, from a book

—**CYRIL CONNOLLY**

Objectional people are numerous. They have one trait in common, that is a most unfortunate tendency to longevity.

—**J. CHALMERS DA COSTA**

Those who in their youth did not live in self-harmony, and who did not gain the true treasures of life, are later like long-legged old herons standing sadly by a lake without fish.

—The **DHAMMAPADA**, probably 3rd century B.C.

Man reaches the highest point of lovableness at twelve to seventeen—to get it back, in a second flowering, at the age of seventy to ninety.

—**ISAK DINESEN**

Women are most fascinating between the ages of thirty-five and forty, after they have won a few races and know how to pace themselves. Since few women ever pass forty maximum fascination can continue indefinitely.

—CHRISTIAN DIOR

The dusky P.M. of our common existence.

—LEON EDEL

I'm saving that rocker for the day when I feel as old as I really am.

—DWIGHT D. EISENHOWER

In every animal that walks upright the deficiency of the fluids that fill the muscles appears first in the highest part. The face first grows lank and wrinkled; then the neck; then the breast and arms; then the lower parts continuing to the last as plump as ever; so that covering all above with a basket, and regarding only what is below the girdle, it is impossible of two women to tell an old one from a young one.

—BENJAMIN FRANKLIN

The injunction to respect age stems from periods when long lives were exceptional.

—MAX FRISCH

Measurement of life should be proportioned rather to the intensity of the experience than to its actual length.

—**THOMAS HARDY**

Men are like wine—some turn to vinegar, but the best improve with age.

—**POPE JOHN XXIII**

[Richard] Ingrams has created a serial version of what we imagine the senescent mind to be: rambling, eccentric, snobbish, alternating between furious dignity and wild silliness, with odd penetrating shafts of hindsight, perspective and reminiscence.

—**NICHOLAS LEZARD**

Old people, sometimes, are the ones who become young, know, are aware, act, believe, and are gay. And get things done.

—**LE CORBUSIER**

One of the two things that men who have lasted for a hundred years always say: either that they have drunk whisky and smoked all their lives, or that neither tobacco nor spirits ever made the faintest appeal to them.

—**E. V. LUCAS**

Old age is like a plane flying through storm. Once you're aboard there's nothing you can do.

—**GOLDA MEIR**

We "become" twenty-one, "turn" thirty, "push" forty, "reach" fifty, "make it" to sixty, and "hit" seventy. If we reach one hundred, we're likely to revert to childhood, proudly adding fractions to the numbers.

—**LARRY MILLER**

A ready means of being cherished by the English is to adopt the simple expedient of living a long time. I have little doubt that if, say, Oscar Wilde had lived into his nineties, instead of dying in his forties, he would have been considered a benign, distinguished figure suitable to preside at a school prize-giving or to instruct and exhort scout-masters at their jamborees. He might even have been knighted.

—**MALCOLM MUGGERIDGE**

Women, as they grow older, rely more and more on cosmetics. Men, as they grow older, rely more and more on a sense of humor.

—**GEORGE JEAN NATHAN**

Success should come late in life in order to compensate for the loss of youth.

—HAROLD NICOLSON

Maturity—to have reacquired the seriousness that one had as a child at play.

—FRIEDRICH W. NIETZSCHE

It gives me great pleasure to converse with the aged. They have been over the road that all of us must travel, and know where it is rough and difficult and where it is level and easy.

—PLATO

It is after you have lost your teeth that you can afford to buy steaks.

—PIERRE AUGUSTE RENOIR

Nothing is more beautiful than cheerfulness in an old face.

—JEAN PAUL RICHTER

I shall be old and ugly some day and I shall look for man's chivalrous help, but I shall not find it. The bees are very attentive to the flowers till their honey is done, and then they fly over them.

—OLIVE SCHREINER

Devotion to an old crock like me is sentimental folly.

[F]or the past week I have had over one hundred congratulations a day. But for two strong men who have worked hard tearing them up for me I should never have been ninety.

—**GEORGE BERNARD SHAW,** letter on his 90th birthday

When a man retires and time is no longer a matter of urgent importance, his colleagues generally present him with a watch.

—**R. C. SHERRIFF**

Every man desires to live long, but no man would be old.

—**JONATHAN SWIFT**

Strangely enough the aged have a lot in common with youth; they are largely unemployed, introspective, and often depressed; their bodies and psyches are in the process of change, and they are heavy users of drugs. If they want to marry, their families tend to disapprove. Both groups are obsessed with time. Youth, however, figures its passage from birth; the aged calculate backward from their death day.

—*TIME* **MAGAZINE**

Consider well the proportions of things. It is better to be a young June-bug than an old bird of paradise.

Methuselah lived to be 969 years old. . . . You boys and girls will see more in the next fifty years than Methuselah saw in his whole lifetime.

—**MARK TWAIN**

> *Methuselah lived nine hundred years,*
> *Methuselah lived nine hundred years;*
> *But who calls that livin'*
> *When no gal will give in,*
> *To no man who's nine hundred years?*

—**IRA GERSHWIN**, *Porgy and Bess*

Old age is the only disease that you don't look forward to being cured of.

—**ORSON WELLES**, *Citizen Kane*

There is nothing like youth. The middle-aged are mort-gaged to Life. The old are in life's lumber room. . . . To win back my youth . . . there is nothing I wouldn't do—except take exercise, get up early, or be a useful member of the community.

The soul is born old, but grows young. That is the comedy of life. The body is born young and grows old. That is life's tragedy.

—OSCAR WILDE

What a cunning and insidious thing, in its approach, is old age! How it steals upon you in the night! How carefully it looks you over before it strikes! Confronting you like a cunning antagonist, it fences cautiously until it sees where your guard is weak; it toys and feels with its point, for some opening where, in careless youth, you removed the shield of health and did not replace it; and then, when the spot is found, with quick and unerring thrust, it pinks you.

—JOHN SERGEANT WISE

He was either a man of about a hundred and fifty who was rather young for his years, or a man of about a hundred and ten who had been aged by trouble.

—P. G. WODEHOUSE

# 10

Rx . . .

Eat a lobster! Eat a

pound of caviar—

live!"

It isn't how long you stick around but what you put over while you are here.

—**George Ade**

Old men are always young enough to learn, with profit.

—**Aeschylus**

To keep the heart unwrinkled, to be hopeful, kindly, cheerful, reverent—that is to triumph over old age.

—**Thomas Bailey Aldrich**

To know how to grow old is the masterwork of wisdom, and one of the most difficult chapters in the great art of living.

—**Henri Frederic Amiel**

There is no such thing as "on the way out." As long as you are still doing something interesting and good, you're in business because you're still breathing.

—**Louis Armstrong**

I would willingly stand at street corners, hat in hand, begging passersby to drop their unused minutes into it.

—**Bernard Berenson**

Maturity is a frank acceptance of barren realities.

—EUGENE F. BRUSSELL

I'll keep going till my face falls off.

—BARBARA CARTLAND

Nothing is more enjoyable than a leisured old age. That is, if one has a reserve of study and learning.

—CICERO, *De Senectute*

Infidelity, that infallible rejuvenator, calms the fear of growing old.

—CYRIL CONNOLLY

Don't put up with being addressed by nurses, aides, and others as "Granny," "Pop," or the like. Point out acidly that you have a name and if they don't know it they can damn well ask and that you were earning a living when they were still eating baby food.

—DR. ALEX COMFORT

The whole business of marshaling one's energies becomes more and more important as one grows older.

—HUME CRONYN

We are not making sufficient demands upon older people. What they want is not idleness and freedom, but an opportunity to do something with their lives that will make them significant.

—**LAWRENCE K. FRANK**

I was still learning when I taught my last class.

—**CLAUDE M. FUESS**

The fact remains that unless one hopes that tomorrow will be more exciting than today, and that next week will be more exciting still, it's rather futile to go on living after fifty, especially in this torn world.

—**SIR JOHN GIELGUD**

No skill or art is needed to grow old; the trick is to endure it.

—**GOETHE**

Long life is the right mode for some people and not for others—just as some people write books in ten volumes and others epigrams in two lines—and the two works may be exactly equal value.

—**FREDERICK GOODYEAR**

Most people say that you get old, you have to give up things. I think you get old because you give up things.

—**SENATOR THEODORE F. GREEN**, at 87

Be wise in time and turn loose the aging horse, lest at last he stumble amid jeers and burst his wind.

—**HORACE**

He that would pass the latter part of life with honor and decency must, when he is young, consider that he shall one day be old; and remember, when he is old, that he has once been young.

At seventy-seven it is time to be earnest.

—**SAMUEL JOHNSON**

For the aging person it is a duty and a necessity to give serious attention to himself.

The afternoon of a human life must have a significance of its own, and cannot be merely a pitiful appendage to life's morning.

—CARL JUNG

• • • • • • • • • • • •

I am old enough to see how little I have done in so much time, and how much I have to do in so little.

—SHEILA KAYE-SMITH

For the last third of life there remains only work. It alone is always stimulating, rejuvenating, exciting, and satisfying.

—KÄTHE KOLLWITZ

Older people are neglected and left to get along as best they can. . . . If it is important to give the human animal a good start in life, it is just as important to see that he makes a good finish. We should be as much interested in actual fulfillment as in setting the stage for the realization of possibilities.

—GEORGE E. LAWTON

Nothing makes one old so quickly as the ever-present thought that one is growing older.

—GEORG CHRISTOPH LICHTENBERG

I really think that it's better to retire, in Uncle Earl's [Long's] terms, when you still have some snap left in your garters.

—SENATOR RUSSELL B. LONG

Growing old is a bad habit which a busy man has no time to form.

—ANDRÉ MAUROIS

The thing is to become a master and in your old age to acquire the courage to do what children did when they knew nothing.

—HENRY MILLER

Tis a maxim with me to be as young as long as I can; there is nothing can pay one for the invaluable ignorance which is the companion of youth; those sanguine groundless hopes, and that lively vanity, which makes all the happiness of life. To my extreme mortification I grow wiser every day.

—LADY MARY WORTLEY MONTAGU

There are so many sorts of defects in old age, so much imbecility, and it is so liable to contempt, that the best acquisition a man can make is the kindness and affection of his own family; command and fear are no longer his weapons.

—MONTAIGNE

I never feel age. . . . If you have creative work, you don't have age or time.

—LOUISE NEVELSON

•

## SATCHEL PAIGE'S GUIDE TO LONGEVITY

1. Avoid fried meats, which angry up the blood.
2. If your stomach disputes you, lie down and pacify it with cool thoughts.
3. Keep the juices flowing by jangling around gently as you move.
4. Go very light on the vices, such as carrying on in society. The social rumble ain't restful.
5. Avoid running at all times.
6. Don't look back. Something might be gaining on you.

•

The belief that youth is the happiest time of life is founded on a fallacy. The happiest person is the person who thinks the most interesting thoughts, and we grow happier as we grow older.

—WILLIAM LYON PHELPS

What good are vitamins? Eat a lobster, eat a pound of caviar—live! If you are in love with a beautiful blonde with an empty face and no brains at all, don't be afraid. Marry her! Live!

—ARTHUR RUBINSTEIN

I have often noticed that a kindly, placid good-humor is the companion of longevity, and, I suspect, frequently the leading cause of it.

—SIR WALTER SCOTT

The crucial task of old age is balance; keeping just well enough, just brave enough, just gay and interested and starkly honest enough to remain a sentient human being.

—FLORIDA SCOTT-MAXWELL

Let me advise thee not to talk of thyself as being old. There is something in Mind Curse, after all, and if thee continually talk of thyself as being old, thee may perhaps bring on some of the infirmities of age. At least I would not risk it if I were thee.

—HANNAH WHITALL SMITH

There are so few who can grow old with a good grace.

—RICHARD STEELE

Retiring must not mean just vegetating. I don't think anybody can do that.

—EDWARD STEICHEN

The most important thing we have learned about the aged is the necessity to give them the shortest possible period "down," the longest period "up." When a patient is "up" he is a citizen, and individual. When he is "down," he and his doctor are in trouble. . . . "Down" is bad, "up" is life.

—DR. MARTIN R. STEINBERG

Dignity, high station, or great riches, are in some sort necessary to old men, in order to keep the younger at a distance, who are otherwise too apt to insult them upon the score of their age.

—JONATHAN SWIFT

Solitude is ill-suited to old age, and the course of circumstances tends too often to leave the old in solitude.

—SIR HENRY TAYLOR

*Old age should burn and rave at close of day;*
*Rage, rage against the dying of the light.*

—DYLAN THOMAS, "Do not Go Gentle Into That Good Night"

From birth to age eighteen, a girl needs good parents, from eighteen to thirty-five she needs good looks, from thirty-five to fifty-five she needs a good personality, and from fifty-five on she needs cash.

—SOPHIE TUCKER

Life should begin with age and its privileges and accumu-
lations, and end with youth and its capacity to splendidly
enjoy such advantages.

—MARK TWAIN

Old age is no such uncomfortable thing, if one gives one
up to it with good grace, and don't drag it about to
midnight dances and the public show.
    If one stays quietly in one's own house in the country,
and cares for nothing but oneself, scolds one's servants,
condemns everything that is new, and recollects how
charming a thousand things were formerly that were very
disagreeable, one gets over the winters very well, and the
summers get over themselves.

—HORACE WALPOLE

You end up as you deserve. In old age you must put up
with the face, the friends, the health, and the children
you have earned.

—FAY WELDON

When we grow old, and our own spirits decay, it reani-
mates one to have a number of living creatures about
one, and to be much with them.

—JOHN WILMOT, Earl of Rochester

[T]he knowledge that death is not far away . . . has the effect of making earthly affairs seem unimportant. . . . And [it is] harder to take human life seriously, including one's own passions and achievements and efforts.

—EDMUND WILSON

O how you hate old age—well so do I. . . . But I, who am more a rebel against man than you, rebel less against nature, and accept the inevitable and go with it gently into the unknown.

—MAUDE GONNE, letter to William Butler Yeats

# 11

# TELLING LIES

"...actually, it's

Mama."

I refuse to admit I'm more than fifty-two even if that does make my sons illegitimate.

—**VISCOUNTESS NANCY ASTOR**

The secret of staying young is to live honestly, eat slowly, and lie about your age.

—**LUCILLE BALL**

A woman's always younger than a man of equal years.

—**ELIZABETH BARRETT BROWNING**

"A very old twelve."

—**NOEL COWARD,** reply when asked how old a certain society lady looked after her most recent facelift

I lied to everybody. I lie very well, being an actress, naturally.

—**LYNN FONTANNE,** on her refusal to reveal her true age, even to her husband Alfred Lunt

You'll never get her to admit it but actually it's Mama.

—**ZSA ZSA GABOR,** when asked which of the famous Gabor women was the oldest.

What's the point? My face, shall we say, looks lived in.

—**AVA GARDNER,** on not lying about her upcoming
65th birthday

Discussing how old you are is the temple of boredom.

—**RUTH GORDON**

Suicide may in fact be an attempt to escape death, shortcut the dreadful deteriorating processes, abort one's natural trajectory, elude "the ruffian on the stairs," in A. E. Housman's phrase for a cruelly painful and anarchic death—make it neat and not messy.

—**EDWARD HOAGLAND**

Allow me to put the record straight. I am forty-six and have been for some years past.

—**ERICA JONG**

Why? I've worked for every damn line in this face!

—**ANNA MAGNANI,** when asked why she never
had a face lift

When a woman tells you her age it's all right to look surprised, but don't scowl.

—**WILSON MIZENER**

I'm sixty-five, I'll be sixty-six in January. What should I do? Shoot myself? I've never worried about age. If you're extremely, painfully frightened of age, it shows. Life doesn't end at thirty. To me age is a number, just a number. Who cares?

—JEANNE MOREAU

How old would you be if you didn't know how old you was?

—SATCHEL PAIGE

Everyone is the age he has decided on, and I have decided to remain thirty years old.

—PABLO PICASSO

The years that a woman subtracts from her age are not lost. They are added to the ages of other women.

—DIANE DE POTIERS

I have always felt that a woman has the right to treat the subject of her age with ambiguity until, perhaps, she passes the realm of over ninety. Then it is better she be candid with herself and the world.

—HELENA RUBINSTEIN

My voice had a long, nonstop career. It deserves to be put to bed with quiet and dignity, not yanked out every once in a while to see if it can still do what it used to do. It can't.

—**BEVERLY SILLS,** on refusal to sing after her retirement from opera

I'd like to go on being thirty-five for a long time.

—**MARGARET THATCHER,** in 1961

No woman should ever be quite accurate about her age. It looks so calculating.

(Lady Bracknell in *The Importance of Being Earnest*)

One should never trust a woman who tells one her real age. A woman who would tell one that, would tell one anything.

Thirty-five is a very attractive age, London society is full of women of the very highest birth who have, of their own free choice, remained thirty-five for years.

—**OSCAR WILDE**

# 12

# Proverbs
# AND TOASTS

• • • • • • • • • • • • • • •

"... when the children

are out of the house

and the dog is dead."

• • • • • • • • • • • •
All the passions are extinguished with old age; self-love never dies.

Age gives good advice when it is no longer able to give bad example.

Age mellows some people; others it makes rotten.

—American proverb
• • • • • • • • • • •

Here's to living it up as long as we can live it down.

—American toast

• • • • • • • • • • •
Life begins neither at conception nor at birth; it starts when the children are out of the house and the dog is dead.

One of the secrets of a long and fruitful life is to forgive everybody everything every night before you go to bed.

Do not resist growing old—many are denied the privilege.

—anonymous
• • • • • • • • • • •

May you live as long as you want, and want to as long as you live.

—anonymous toast

Fifty is a good age, because when a woman says "yes," you're flattered, and when she says "no," you're relieved.

—French saying

An old barn burns high.

Old age and poverty are two heavy burdens. Either is enough.

—German proverb

Let him live to be a hundred! We want him on earth.

—**OLIVER WENDELL HOLMES JR.**, toast to a friend

You're not as young as you used to be, but you're not as old as you're going to be. So watch it!

In youth we have our troubles before us; in age we leave pleasures behind.

The old man hasn't the place of the cat in the ashes.

—Irish proverb

Everything ripe was once sour.

—Latin proverb

The old hen makes good soup.

—Spanish proverb

If the rich could hire others to die for them, the poor could make a nice living.

Young, a donkey; old, an ass.

As you are at seven, so you are at seventy.

Up to seventy we learn wisdom—and die fools.

Shrouds are made without pockets.

—Yiddish proverb

# 13

# Making the

# BEST OF IT

• • • • • • • • • • • • • •

"I'll keep right on

dancing."

The Indian Summer of life should be a little sunny and a little sad, like the season, and infinite in wealth, and depth of tone—but never hustled.

—HENRY ADAMS

Life is precious to the old person. He is not interested merely in thoughts of yesterday's good life and tomorrow's path to the grave. He does not want his later years to be a sentence of solitary confinement in society. Nor does he want them to be a death watch.

—DR. DAVID ALLMAN

It's sad to grow old, but nice to ripen.

—BRIGITTE BARDOT

Wisdom of the years: "I will not make it difficult for others. Neither will I make it difficult for myself."

—LOUISE BOGAN

Childhood itself is scarcely more lovely than a cheerful, kind, sunshiny old age.

—LYDIA M. CHILD

One does not leave a convivial party before closing time.

—**WINSTON CHURCHILL,** on being asked if he will retire
as prime minister

Grandmother, about eighty, is visiting in the East and sends home things she has bought for her house. "I don't suppose I shall live forever," she says, "but while I do live I don't see why I shouldn't live as if I expected to."

—**CHARLES HORTON COOLEY**

The joy of being older is that in one's life one can, towards the end of the run, overact appallingly.

—**QUENTIN CRISP**

"Then it's eight o'clock and I fight sleep, damn it all. I fight it with everything I've got! I don't want to go to bed, life's too short. Actually, I sleep twelve hours or maybe fourteen. Sleep is my last lover. I don't want it, but there you have it . . . I accept with grace. What else can I do?"

—**BESSIE DOENGES,** at 93

Being young is beautiful, but being old is comfortable.

—**MARIE EBNER-EISENBACH**

I am long on ideas, but short on time. I expect to live to be only about a hundred.

—THOMAS A. EDISON

Very, very, very few people die at ninety-two. I suppose that I shall be safer still at ninety-three.

—WILLARD ESPY

Being an old maid is like death by drowning, a really delightful sensation after you cease to struggle.

—EDNA FERBER

I said, don't celebrate. If I can manage to go on working, it's much more interesting. One of the things one does enjoy in old age is being able to make excuses not to do things you don't want to do.

—SIR JOHN GIELGUD, at 90

Having ceased to regard death as a threat, I now accept it as the last of the many surprises of which my life is the sum.

—JOHN HOUSEMAN

It's a damned nuisance, getting older, but it's not exactly depressing.

—ELSA LANCHESTER

I must not forget to tell you of the death of a fellow of Trinity College aged ninety-seven. His funeral was attended by a brother of ninety-nine. The latter was much distressed and said he had always told his junior that theological research was not compatible with longevity. "God," he solemnly told Rutherford, "does not mean us to pry into these matters." After the funeral the old man went back to Trinity and solemnly drank his half-bottle of port. He was asked his prescription for health and said with great fervour, "Never deny yourself anything." He explained that he had never married as he had found fidelity restrictive as a young man. "I was once engaged, when I was forty." he said. "And I found it gave me very serious constipation. So I broke off the engagement and the lady quite understood." He was very anxious not to be thought past the age of flirtation.

—HAROLD J. LASKI

The great thing about getting older is that you don't lose all the other ages you've been.

—MADELEINE L'ENGLE

I want to die young at a ripe old age.

—Ashley Montagu

I prefer to forget both pairs of glasses and to pass my declining years saluting strange women and grandfather clocks.

—Ogden Nash

When one has reached eighty-one one likes to sit back and let the world turn by itself, without trying to push it.

—Sean O'Casey

If by the time we're sixty we haven't learned what a knot of paradox and contradiction life is, and how exquisitely the good and the bad are mingled in every action we take, and what a compromising hostess Our Lady of Truth is, we haven't grown old to much purpose.

—John Cowper Powys

I live in a valley below Grasse in a cottage enclosed by cypresses. Behind me loom the hills where the walls are perched in the sunlight. Below me flows the cold green canal of the Siagne. Every morning I look at the dew which clings to the olive trees and I wonder what strange new excitement the day will hold for me. . . . My voyage is at its end. I think how glorious to grow old!

—Frederic Prokosch, Voices: A Memoir

The advantage of being eighty years old is that one has had many people to love.

—JEAN RENOIR

I won't be old till my feet hurt, and they only hurt when I don't let 'em dance enough, so I'll keep right on dancing.

—BILL "BOJANGLES" ROBINSON

I agree that the last years of life are the best, if one is a philosopher.

—GEORGE SANTAYANA

Paradoxical as it may seem, to believe in youth is to look backward; to look forward we must believe in age.

—DOROTHY L. SAYERS

Let us cherish and love old age, for it is full of pleasure if we know how to use it.

—SENECA

Growing old—it's not nice, but it's interesting.

—AUGUST STRINDBERG

Whatever a man's age, he can reduce it several years by putting a bright-colored flower in his buttonhole.

—**MARK TWAIN**

In spite of illness, in spite of the archenemy sorrow, one *can* remain alive long past the usual date of disintegration if one is unafraid of change, insatiable in intellectual curiosity, interested in big things, and happy in small ways.

—**EDITH WHARTON**

*An aged man is but a paltry thing.*
*A tattered coat upon a stick,*
*unless soul clap its hands and sing.*

("Sailing to Byzantium")

*Though leaves are many, the root is one;*
*Through all the lying days of my youth*
*I swayed my leaves and flowers in the sun;*
*Now I may wither into the truth.*

—**WILLIAM BUTLER YEATS,** "A Drinking Song"